# Dip the Chip!

**Kelly Doudna**

Consulting Editor, Diane Craig, M.A./Reading Specialist

Published by ABDO Publishing Company, 4940 Viking Drive, Edina, Minnesota 55435.

Printed in the United States.

Credits
Edited by: Pam Price
Curriculum Coordinator: Nancy Tuminelly
Cover and Interior Design and Production: Mighty Media
Photo Credits: Comstock, Kelly Doudna, Wewerka Photography

Library of Congress Cataloging-in-Publication Data

Doudna, Kelly, 1963-
    Dip the chip! / Kelly Doudna.
        p. cm. -- (First rhymes)
    Includes index.
    ISBN 1-59679-469-0 (hardcover)
    ISBN 1-59679-470-4 (paperback)
        1. English language--Rhyme--Juvenile literature. I. Title. II. Series.
PE1517.D6267 2006
808.1--dc22

                                                                        2005049157

SandCastle™ books are created by a professional team of educators, reading specialists, and content developers around five essential components that include phonemic awareness, phonics, vocabulary, text comprehension, and fluency. All books are written, reviewed, and leveled for guided reading and early intervention reading, and designed for use in shared, guided, and independent reading and writing activities to support a balanced approach to literacy instruction.

# Let Us Know

After reading the book, SandCastle would like you to tell us your stories about reading. What is your favorite page? Was there something hard that you needed help with? Share the ups and downs of learning to read. We want to hear from you! To get posted on the ABDO Publishing Company Web site, send us e-mail at:

**sandcastle@abdopub.com**

**SandCastle Level: Beginning**

# -ip

chip

dip

flip

lip

tip

See the .

Look at the .

She does a .

Here is her  .

This is the .

This chip is big.

The dip is good.

# A flip is fun.

Her lip is pink.

# The tip is small.

# Dip the Chip!

Kim has a potato chip.

Kim wants to dip her chip.

Kim puts the tip
of her chip
into the dip.

When Kim eats the chip
some of the dip
from the tip of the chip
gets on her lip.

Kim likes the dip
on her lip
from the tip
of the chip,
so she does a flip!

# About SandCastle™

A professional team of educators, reading specialists, and content developers created the SandCastle™ series to support young readers as they develop reading skills and strategies and increase their general knowledge. The SandCastle™ series has four levels that correspond to early literacy development in young children. The levels are provided to help teachers and parents select the appropriate books for young readers.

**Emerging Readers**
(no flags)

**Beginning Readers**
(1 flag)

**Transitional Readers**
(2 flags)

**Fluent Readers**
(3 flags)

These levels are meant only as a guide. All levels are subject to change.

To see a complete list of SandCastle™ books and other nonfiction titles from ABDO Publishing Company, visit www.abdopub.com or contact us at:
4940 Viking Drive, Edina, Minnesota 55435 • 1-800-800-1312 • fax: 1-952-831-1632